Discover Sharks

WHALE
SHARK

Camilla de la Bédoyère

QED Publishing

First published in the UK in 2012 by
QED Publishing
A Quarto Group company
230 City Road
London EC1V 2TT

www.qed-publishing.co.uk

A catalogue record for this book is available from
the British Library.

ISBN 978 1 78171 073 9

Printed in China

Consultant Mary Lindeed
Editor Tasha Percy
Designer Melissa Alaverdy

Words in **bold**
are explained
in the Glossary
on page 24

CONTENTS

WHAT IS A WHALE SHARK?

Whale sharks
are big **fish**.
They live
in oceans.

These big sharks swim in warm water.

Whale sharks often swim near people but do not attack them.

GENTLE GIANTS

Whale sharks are the biggest sharks in the world. They are also the biggest fish in the world.

Whale sharks can grow up to 20 metres long.

A whale shark is as big as a bus!

SPOTTY SKIN

Look at the whale shark's skin. It is dark blue-green on the top.

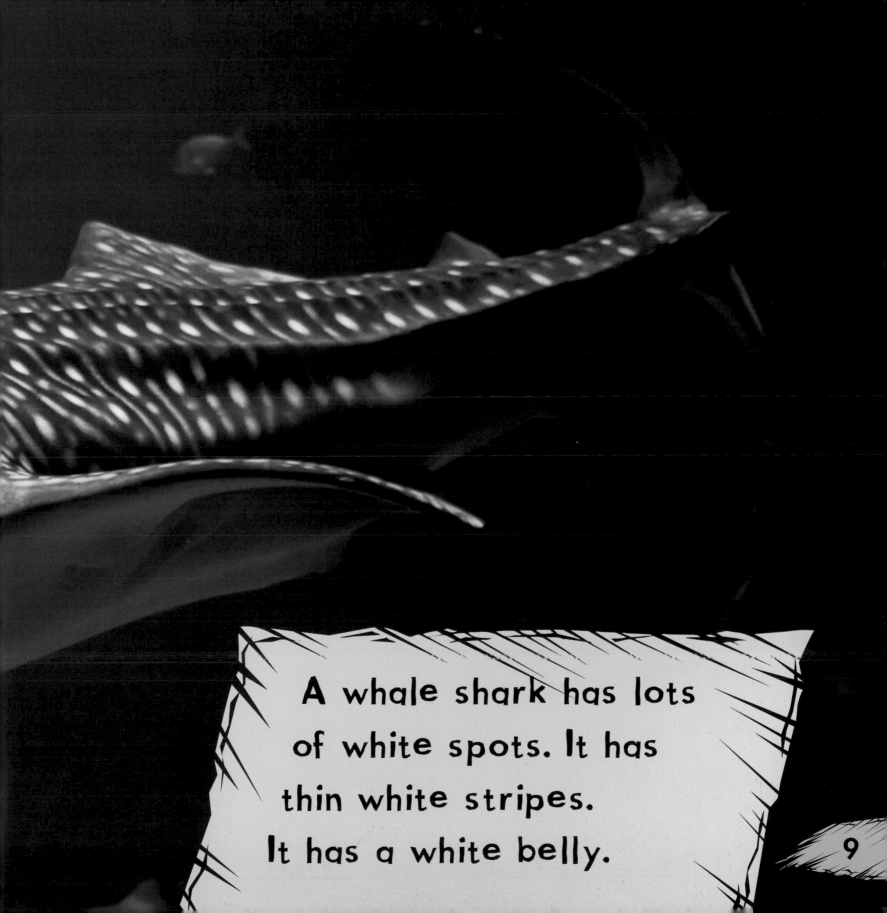

A whale shark has lots
of white spots. It has
thin white stripes.
It has a white belly.

9

BIG JAWS

Look at the whale shark's mouth. It is enormous!

teeth |---------

These huge **jaws** can open more than 2 metres wide. There are lots of small teeth.

———— Jaws

GULPING FOOD

The shark swims with its mouth open. Water and small animals go into its mouth.

The shark eats the small animals. The water comes back out of its **gills**.

A whale shark gulps its food.

gills

SNACK ATTACK

Whale sharks do not hunt big animals. They eat small animals that float or swim.

krill |- - - - - - -

jellyfish

Whale sharks eat
krill, small fish, squid
and jellyfish.

squid |- - - - - -

15

SWIMMING FAR

Most sharks swim fast.
Whale sharks swim slowly.

They can swim far across
the world. Others stay...

Fins help the shark swim.

TIME FOR SCHOOL

These sharks are eating fish eggs.

Most sharks live alone. Whale sharks sometimes swim in groups.

They swim in a **school** when they are eating.

19

WHALE SHARKS AND US

Sometimes whale sharks swim where there are people. These huge fish do not attack humans.

Some whale sharks
are even friendly!
It's great to watch
one swimming
nearby.

Now we know that whale sharks are amazing animals!

GLOSSARY

fin   a part on the body of a fish shaped like a flap, used for moving and steering through the water

fish   a cold-blooded animal that lives in water and has scales, fins and gills

gill   the part of the body on a fish's side through which it breathes

jaws   the two bones in the face that hold the teeth

krill   a tiny ocean animal that looks like a shrimp

school   a group of fish or other sea animals

shark   a large and often fierce fish that feeds on meat and has very sharp teeth